cl**o**verleaf books™

Fall and Winter Holidays

Caleb's Hanukkah

Lisa Bullard

illustrated by **Constanza Basaluzzo**

M MILLBROOK PRESS • MINNEAPOLIS

For Emmett —L.B.

For Agus, Milli, Mica,
Lauren, and Joa —C.B.

Millbrook Press
A division of Lerner Publishing Group, Inc.
241 First Avenue North
Minneapolis, MN 55401 U.S.A.

Website address: www.lernerbooks.com

Main body text set in Slappy Inline 18/28.
Typeface provided by T26.

Library of Congress Cataloging-in-Publication Data

Bullard, Lisa.
    Caleb's Hanukkah / by Lisa Bullard ; illustrated by
Constanza Basaluzzo.
        p.   cm. — (Cloverleaf books. Fall and winter holidays)
    Includes index.
    ISBN 978-0-7613-5077-4 (lib bdg. : alk. paper)
    1. Hanukkah—Juvenile literature. I. Basaluzzo, Constanza.
II. Title.
BM695.H3B85 2013
296.4'35—dc23   2011051539

Manufactured in the United States of America
1 – PP – 7/15/12

TABLE OF CONTENTS

Chapter One

The Hanukkah Story

Hi, I'm Caleb! See this **dreidel** I'm spinning? We play a game with it for **Hanukkah.**

Hanukkah lasts for eight nights. It usually takes place during December. The timing is based on the Jewish calendar.

I keep spinning while Dad tells me the Hanukkah story.
It happened over **two thousand years** ago.

Hanukkah began in the city of Jerusalem. It is in the country now called Israel. In modern times, Jewish people all over the world celebrate Hanukkah.

A Greek king named Antiochus IV made it against the law to practice the Jewish religion. He took over the Jewish Temple in Jerusalem.

Some Jewish people fought back. Their army was much smaller than the king's.

But they beat the king's big army. They took back their temple. They were free to practice their religion!

The Jewish people were not supposed to study their religion. But they got together to do it anyway. Sometimes the king's soldiers saw them studying in groups. Stories say the Jewish people then pretended they were just playing dreidel. Dreidels helped them keep their secret!

Chapter Two

A Miracle Happened

Dad says the Jewish people cleaned the temple so they could use it again. They lit the temple's **special oil lamp**. But there was only enough oil to light the lamp for one day.

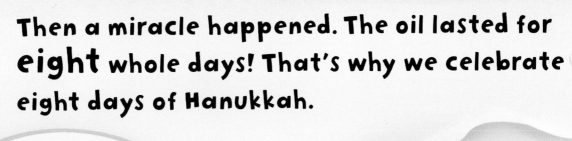

Then a miracle happened. The oil lasted for **eight** whole days! That's why we celebrate eight days of Hanukkah.

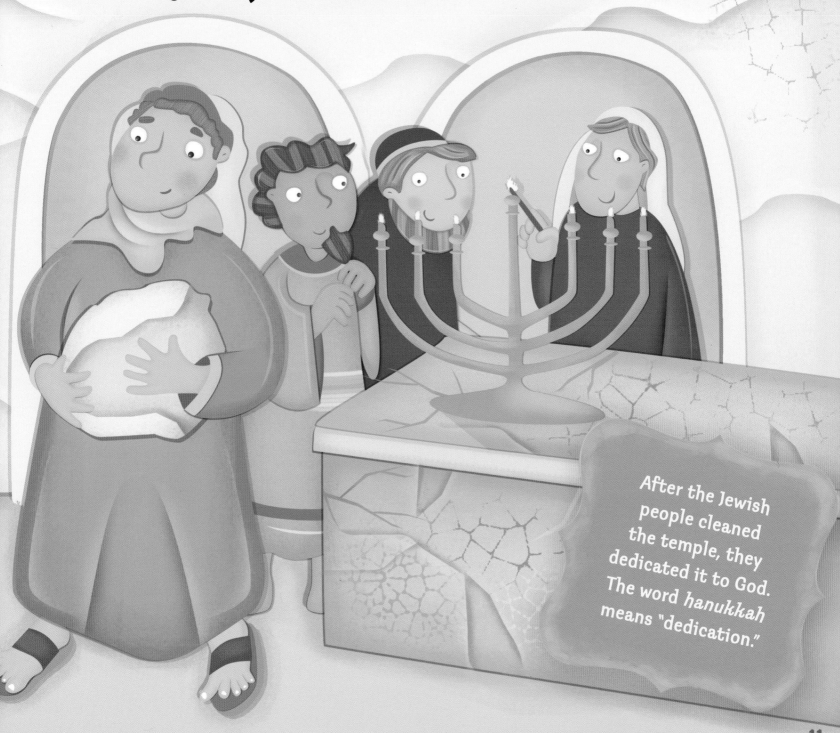

After the Jewish people cleaned the temple, they dedicated it to God. The word *hanukkah* means "dedication."

These marks on my dreidel are **Hebrew** letters. Dad says they stand for "A great miracle happened there."

The letters on dreidels in Israel stand for "A great miracle happened here."

I bet another great thing is going to happen tonight. I'm finally going to win the game!

Chapter Three

Lighting the Candles

Relatives come to **celebrate** with us. The sun sets. We say blessings to God. We use a helper candle to light the first candle.

Each night of **Hanukkah**, we'll add another **candle.**

Hanukkah is also called the Festival of Lights. People light the menorah each night. It holds a candle for each day of Hanukkah, plus the helper candle. Families often put their menorah in a window. They want everyone to see it.

We sing together. Then the kids get Hanukkah **gelt** as presents! That's money. Some of the coins are chocolate. Some of the money is real.

Many children receive gifts for Hanukkah. Some share what they are given with others. Sharing with those in need is part of the Jewish religion.

I'll share some of mine. I'll give it to
people who need it more than I do.

Then we eat the **latkes**. Those are potato pancakes. We always have them for Hanukkah. Mom fries them in hot oil. The **oil** reminds us of the miracle.

People in Israel usually eat jelly doughnuts instead of latkes. Doughnuts are fried in oil too.

19

Chapter Four

Dreidel Time!

Finally, it's dreidel time. We all take turns spinning. I win a big pile of **chocolate coins!** I'll share those too.

People use coins, chocolate, and other items as game pieces in dreidel. Players take turns spinning. The Hebrew letter that lands up tells what happens next. A player might have to put a game piece in the middle. Or he or she might win everything from the middle. The one to get all the pieces is the winner!

There are seven more nights of Hanukkah. That's seven more nights of dreidel to help us celebrate!

Make a Milk Carton Dreidel

What you will need:

empty 8-oz. milk carton
sharp knife (to be used only by a grown-up)
sharp scissors (to be used only by a grown-up)

Popsicle stick
blue masking tape (painter's tape)
black permanent marker

Make your dreidel:

1) Open the top of your milk carton completely. Wash the inside and outside of your milk carton. Let it dry.

2) Ask a grown-up to cut each side of the carton top into a triangle that points up. The tops of the triangles should meet in the middle. They will form a pointy end for your dreidel. Tape the sides of the triangles together.

3) Ask the grown-up to also cut a Popsicle stick-sized slit in the bottom center of the carton.

4) Poke your Popsicle stick up through the hole. Leave some of the stick outside the box so you can use it as a spinning handle.

5) Cover the entire carton with the blue masking tape.

6) The four Hebrew letters found on dreidels are shown below. Draw one on each side of your top using the permanent marker.

נ   ג   ה   שׁ

Nun   Gimel   Hey   Shin

Now you are ready to play the dreidel game! Find the rules of the game on the Web at http://www.dreidel.com/rules.php.

Antiochus IV (an-tee-AH-kuss the fourth): a king who ruled over the Jewish people more than two thousand years ago. He made it against the law to study or practice the Jewish religion.

celebrate: do something to show how special or important something is

dedicate (DED-ih-kayt): to set apart for a special use

dreidel (DRAY-duhl): a four-sided spinning top

gelt: a word for money in the Yiddish language

Hanukkah (HAH-noo-kuh): a Jewish holiday, from the Hebrew word for "dedication." It can also be spelled many other ways, including Chanukah, Chanukkah, Hanuka, or Channuka.

Hebrew (HEE-broo): the language of the Jewish people

Jewish: related to the religion called Judaism or to the people known as Jews

Jewish Temple: a special place for Jewish people to worship in old Jerusalem

latke (LAHT-kuh): the word for pancake in the Yiddish language, especially a pancake made of potatoes

menorah (meh-NOR-uh): a special candleholder used in the Jewish religion

miracle: an event that can't be explained by science or facts, that people sometimes say happened because of their god or gods

religion: a set of beliefs in a god or gods

BOOKS

Adler, David A. *The Story of Hanukkah.* New York: Holiday House, 2011.
This book tells the story of how Hanukkah began and teaches you how to make latkes and play dreidel.

Heiligman, Deborah. *Celebrate Hanukkah with Lights, Latkes, and Dreidels.*
Washington, DC: National Geographic, 2006.
This book tells more about how Jewish people around the world celebrate Hanukkah.

Balsley, Tilda. *Maccabee!: The Story of Hanukkah.* Minneapolis: Kar-Ben, 2010.
In this rhyming story, Judah and his army of Maccabees fight to free the Jewish people from King Antiochus. Find out more about the first Hanukkah.

WEBSITES

Chanukah
http://www.chabad.org/kids/article_cdo/aid/354748/jewish/Chanukah.htm
At this website from Chabad.org, you will find videos, stories, songs, and games for Hanukkah.

Hanukkah for Children
http://www.akhlah.com/holidays/hanukkah/hanukkah.php
This website from Akhlah has crafts, recipes, blessings, and other ways you can learn more about Hanukkah.

Welcome to the Virtual Dreidel!
http://joi.org/dreidel/index.shtml
This website from the Jewish Outreach Institute lets you play dreidel online.

LERNER e SOURCE™
Expand learning beyond the printed book. Download free, complementary educational resources for this book from our website, www.lerneresource.com.